I BELIEVE IN GOD

THE APOSTLES' CREED

By REV. LAWRENCE G. LOVASIK, S.V.D.
Divine Word Missionary

CATHOLIC BOOK PUBLISHING CORP.
TOTOWA, NJ

Nihil Obstat: Daniel V. Flynn, J.C.D., *Censor Librorum*
Imprimatur: ✝ James P. Mahoney, D.D., *Vicar General, Archdiocese of New York*

CPSIA   December 2010   10 9 8 7 6 5 4 3 2   A/P

The Apostles' Creed

GOD THE FATHER

I BELIEVE IN GOD, the Father Almighty,
Creator of heaven and earth.

GOD THE SON

AND IN JESUS CHRIST,
His only Son, our Lord,
Who was conceived by the Holy Spirit,
born of the Virgin Mary,
suffered under Pontius Pilate,
was crucified,
died and was buried.
He descended into hell;
the third day He arose again from the dead;
He ascended into heaven,
sits at the right hand of God,
the Father Almighty;
from thence He shall come to judge
the living and the dead.

GOD THE HOLY SPIRIT

I BELIEVE IN THE HOLY SPIRIT,
the Holy Catholic Church,
the Communion of Saints,
the forgiveness of sins,
the resurrection of the body,
and life everlasting. Amen.

GOD THE FATHER

God the Creator

"I believe in God, the Father Almighty, Creator of heaven and earth . . ."

THERE are three Persons in God: the Father, the Son, and the Holy Spirit. The Holy Trinity means one God in three Persons. God is the highest Being. God always was, and He always will be. From Him all things come. He made everything that is. Nothing can be without Him.

There can be only one God, and He is a Spirit. He does not have a body as we have.

3

AN ANGEL is a person. An Angel is a spirit, a being that can know and love and want, but without a body.

God made the Angels. Some of the Angels did not do what God told them. They had to be thrown into hell. They are called bad angels, or devils.

The good Angels did what God said. He took them to heaven. The good Angels want to help us to be good.

Each one of us has a Guardian Angel to protect us and to help us to be good.

GOD MADE MAN

GOD made Adam and Eve. They were our first parents. They lived in a beautiful garden. God gave them a great gift called sanctifying grace. It made their souls holy and pleasing to God, and they became His dear children.

A DAM and Eve were very happy in the garden called Paradise because they loved God and were in God's grace. God gave them one command: "You must not eat the fruit of the Tree of Knowledge of good and evil. If you eat of it, you shall die."

Satan was jealous. He told Eve to disobey God and she ate the fruit of the tree and gave some to Adam. Adam and Eve sinned. It is called the original sin because it was the first sin on earth. It is passed on to us.

GOD then told Adam that he would have to work all the days of his life, and that he and his wife would have to die. He told His Angel to send them out of Paradise.

Then God told the devil, who had the form of a snake, that He would send His own Son, Jesus Christ, to fight him and destroy him. Jesus, the Savior of Mankind, would have a Mother, the Blessed Virgin Mary.

GOD THE SON

God Becomes Man

"I believe in Jesus Christ, His only Son, our Lord, Who was conceived by the Holy Spirit, born of the Virgin Mary . . ."

GOD promised to send His Son to make up for our sins and to get back for us that gift of sanctifying grace to make us children of God again.

GOD sent the Angel Gabriel to Nazareth to ask Mary to be the Mother of His Son. The Angel said, "Hail, full of grace, the Lord is with you. Blessed are you among women."

The Angel said, "The Holy Spirit will come upon you and He Who is to be born will be called Son of God."

Mary said, "I am the servant of the Lord. Let it be done to me as you say."

At that moment God became man and Mary became the Mother of God. Through the Holy Spirit Jesus became present in Mary.

The Savior is God the Son, the Second Person of the Blessed Trinity. Jesus Christ is God and Man. He is only one Person, but has two natures: the nature of God and the nature of man. He is the Son of God and the Son of the Blessed Virgin Mary.

THE BIRTH OF JESUS

T HE Roman Emperor Augustus ordered all the people to be counted in the places from which their families had come. Mary and Joseph, being of the family of David, left their home in Nazareth and traveled to Bethlehem.

There was no room in Bethlehem for them, so they had to go to a stable where the animals of travelers were kept. During the night Mary gave birth to her Son, wrapped Him in soft clothes and laid Him in a manger, where the donkeys and oxen were fed.

AN ANGEL appeared to shepherds near Bethlehem and said, "I come to bring you good news of a great joy to be shared by the whole people. This day in David's city a Savior has been born to you, the Messiah and Lord. In a manger you will find an Infant wrapped in swaddling clothes." More Angels appeared, praising God and saying, "Glory to God in high heaven, peace on earth to those on whom His favor rests."

The shepherds went at once and found Mary and Joseph, and the Baby lying in the manger.

Later some learned men, called Magi, arrived in Jerusalem from the east, asking, "Where is the newborn King of the Jews? We saw His star and have come to honor Him." The priests said the Messiah was to be born in Bethlehem. The Magi saw the star again, which led them to the Child and Mary, His Mother. They bowed before Him and gave Him gifts of gold and rich spices.

SOON after the Magi had gone away, God sent an Angel to tell Joseph, the foster father of Jesus, to flee to Egypt because Herod wanted to kill the Child. At once Joseph took the Child and His Mother and left for Egypt. He stayed there until the death of Herod.

An Angel again appeared and told Joseph to take the Child and His Mother and return to the town of Nazareth.

Jesus was obedient to Mary and Joseph. As He became older, He also grew in wisdom and age and grace before God and men. He helped His Mother in the home and learned the trade of a carpenter from Joseph. After Joseph died, Jesus took care of His Mother until He was thirty years old.

THE TIME came when Jesus was grown into a man and had to leave the quiet home of Nazareth and begin His Father's work. He was baptized in the river Jordan by John the Baptist, who heard a voice from heaven, saying, "This is My beloved Son. My favor rests on Him."

After spending forty days in the desert, Jesus began to preach to the people and tell them about the kingdom of God. He said, "Love God with your whole heart, and your neighbor as yourself."

He picked out twelve men to help Him, who were His Apostles and who were to become His first priests. He worked miracles by healing the sick and even raising the dead.

JESUS Christ is the Son of God, the Second Person of the Blessed Trinity Who became man for love of us through the Holy Spirit.

Jesus is our Savior and Redeemer. He invites us all, when He says, "Come to Me, all you who are weary and find life burdensome, and I will refresh you. Take My yoke upon your shoulders, and learn from Me, for I am gentle and humble of heart. Your souls will find rest, for My yoke is easy and My burden light."

"I believe in Jesus Christ, Who suffered under Pontius Pilate . . .

THE night before His death, Jesus gave His Apostles His last instructions and left Himself with us in the Blessed Sacrament. He said to His Apostles, "Take and eat; this is My Body to be given up for you. Do this in remembrance of Me. This cup is the new covenant in My Blood, which will be shed for you."

Later He was captured in the Garden of Gethsemane and led before the high priest for trial. He was then led to Pilate for judgment and was condemned to death.

was crucified, died and was buried."

JESUS carried a Cross to the hill of Calvary where He was nailed to the Cross. He suffered very much for three hours. From the Cross He prayed for those who made Him suffer.

He gave us to the care of His own Mother and offered His soul to His Father when He prayed, "Father, into Your hands I commend My spirit." Jesus died for love of us to take away our sins and to bring us to heaven.

THE RESURRECTION OF JESUS

"I believe in Jesus Christ, Who descended into hell . . ."

WHEN Jesus died on the Cross, His soul went to limbo, where the souls of good people, who died before Jesus came, waited for Him to take them to heaven.

The body of Jesus was lying in the grave for three days.

"The third day He arose again from the dead . . ."

AT DAWN on Sunday morning, all at once
the earth began to tremble and a mighty
Angel of the Lord came down from heaven and
rolled away the stone and sat upon it. Jesus rose
by His own power. His body was beautiful and
able to move about suddenly and freely. He appeared to His friends to make them share in the
joy of His victory.

WOMEN came to the tomb, bringing the spices they had prepared. They found the stone rolled back from the tomb; but when they entered the tomb, they did not find the body of Jesus. Two Angels in white garments said to them, "Why do you search for the Living One among the dead? He is not here; He has been raised up. Remember that He said to you that the Son of Man must be delivered into the hands of sinful men, and be crucified, and on the third day rise again." They told these things to the Apostles.

Jesus also appeared to Mary Magdalene and to His Apostles and disciples. The night of His Resurrection He stood before His Apostles and said, "Peace be with you. As the Father has sent Me, so I send you." Then He breathed on them and said, "Receive the Holy Spirit. If you forgive men's sins, they are forgiven them."

Later Jesus said to Simon Peter, "Simon, son of John, do you love Me more than these?" "Yes, Lord," he said, "You know that I love You." At which Jesus said, "Feed My sheep."

THE ASCENSION OF JESUS

"I believe in Jesus Christ, Who ascended into heaven . . ."

MANY times after He came out of the grave, Jesus appeared to His friends. He once appeared to five hundred of His friends. At another time, when the Apostles were upon a mountain in Galilee, Jesus appeared to them and told them what they must do when He had gone to heaven.

JESUS said, "Full power has been given to Me both in heaven and on earth; go, therefore, and make disciples of all the nations. Baptize them in the name of the Father, and of the Son, and of the Holy Spirit. Teach them to carry out everything I have commanded you. And know that I am with you always."

Jesus also said, "You will receive power when the Holy Spirit comes down on you; then you are to be My witnesses in Jerusalem, yes, even in the whole world." Then He was lifted up before them in a cloud that took Him from their sight.

They were still gazing up into the heavens when two men dressed in white stood beside them. "Men of Galilee," they said, "why do you stand here looking up at the skies? This Jesus Who has been taken from you will return, just as you saw Him go up into the heavens."

"Sits at the right hand of God, the Father Almighty . . ."

A S JESUS took His place beside His heavenly Father, the whole court of heaven gave forth a glorious song of praise.

Jesus is now in heaven as our Eternal High Priest and King, praying for us before His Father and giving us the graces we need to save our soul.

"From thence He shall come to judge the living and the dead . . ."

ON THE last day of this world, our bodies will come back to life, and they will rise from the grave.

And Jesus will come again, with great power and glory, with all the Angels and Saints, to judge all. He will reward the good and punish the wicked.

The Sending of the Holy Spirit

"I believe in the Holy Spirit . . ."

THE Holy Spirit is God and the Third Person of the Blessed Trinity. He makes our soul holy by giving us sanctifying grace. This grace gives us new life—the life of God Himself. It makes us children of God and the temple of the Holy Spirit. It opens heaven for us. The Holy Spirit also gives us grace to help us to be good.

TEN days after Jesus went to heaven, He sent the Holy Spirit to His Church.

The Holy Spirit came in the form of tongues of fire to show His love, and in a great wind to show the power of His grace. He lives in the Catholic Church to guide and help it.

"I believe in the Holy Catholic Church . . ."

THE Catholic Church is the Church of Jesus because He started it, and it teaches everything that Jesus taught. It gives us the grace of the Seven Sacraments, especially the Holy Sacrifice of the Mass.

Jesus gave us the Church to be a sure and true guide to heaven.

Jesus made Saint Peter the head of His Church on earth.

THE Pope in Rome is the head of the Church today. He takes the place of Jesus on earth. All the Bishops are the followers of the Apostles.

The priests help in teaching all people who belong to the Church. They make people holy through the Sacraments and guide them to God.

"I believe in the Communion of Saints . . ."

THE Communion of Saints means that we are all one family of God, loving and helping one another, whether we are on earth, in heaven or in purgatory.

Jesus commands us to love one another. He wants us to be friends with the Saints in heaven by asking for their prayers, and with the souls in purgatory by praying for them.

"I believe in the forgiveness of sins . . ."

JESUS has given His Church the power to forgive sins. He said to Peter, "I will entrust to you the keys of the kingdom of heaven. Whatever you declare bound on earth shall be bound in heaven; whatever you declare loosed on earth shall be loosed in heaven." He said to His Apostles on the evening of Easter day, "If you forgive men's sins, they are forgiven them."

God forgives our sins in the Sacrament of Penance.

"I believe in the resurrection of the body . . ."

A T THE moment the soul leaves the body at death, it is judged by God. God will decide if we go to heaven, purgatory or hell.

A T THE end of the world, Jesus Christ will be on the throne of divine justice. The bodies of all who ever have lived will be raised from the dead and will be united again with their own souls. God will reward the good in His heavenly kingdom. He will punish the wicked in hell.

Jesus once said, "When the Son of Man comes in His glory, with all the Angels of heaven, He will sit upon His royal throne, and all the nations will be gathered before Him. Then He will separate them into two groups. He will say to those on His right: 'Come. You have My Father's blessing! Inherit the kingdom prepared for you from the creation of the world.'" The just will go to eternal life.

Jesus will say to those on His left: "Out of My sight, you condemned, into that everlasting fire prepared for the devil and his angels!" And these will go off to eternal punishment.

"I believe in life everlasting . . ."

JESUS is our one hope for eternal life. We must believe in Him.